Letters to You

Also by Douglas Morea

Poetry

Trials of Substance

The Starling in the Grass Has

Monsters in Bed

Holy Warthog Mamma

How About Meet Me Where Nothing Has Ever Happened in the History of the World

Not Sterilized but You Won't Die From It/The Even Newer Testament

Other

The Andrist: a Sexual Political Essay

Book of Crosses: A Thematic Cartoon Collection

Letters to You

Douglas Morea

BROKEN TURTLE BOOKS LLC
Newark, Delaware

Copyright © 2013 by Douglas Morea
Library of Congress Catalogue Number: 2012945221
ISBN-10:0-9788451-4-5
ISBN-13: 978-0-9788451-4-8
Printed in the United States of America by Lightning Source

Cover Design by Kristina B. Lynn
Butterfly in stamp is derived from Frank Hurley Collection
National Library of Australia (Public Domain)
Book designed by Phillip Bannowsky

SAN 851-7681
Broken Turtle Books LLC
336 N. Dillwyn Road
Newark, DE 19711-5505

FOR MATTHEW GREENSTONE

—dear friend of childhood, who in our adulthood has taught me to share in letters

Contents

AUTHOR'S PRERAMBLE.................... xv
PART 1................................ 1
   Ah Sunflower 3
   Apology to Karen 4
   To the Gordian Knot 5
   To My Digestive Tract 6
   Sir Dinner 7
   Jack as the Being Stalked 8
   Bob Dylan's X-Mas Album (a Review) .. 9
   So a Fly Lands on Your 10
   To the Fly I Just Killed 11
   Take Me Out at the Ball Game 12
   Never Let 13
   Dear Clement C. Moore 14
   To Poe or Not to Poe 15
   Mom 16
   Dad 17
   To Chicken Dinner 18
   Doomsday, What's Your Angle? 19
   Dear Birth 20
   Dear Death 21
   Hey Canada Geese, How Come Your Babies Almost Never Get Run Over Anymore? 22

Advice to Parents 23
Hey Fat Old Man 24
To an Artist as a Young Not
Somebody Yet 25
O Cat 26
Welcome, Plants and Animals
That I Eat 27
To Fear 28
To a Corpse with the Hiccups 29
And So, Fidel 30
O My Sweet-Heart Statue of
Liberty 31
Back 32
Dad? 33
Dear Robert B. 34
Patti Dear? 35
Oh! Liana 36
Liana, Again 37
Why, Stupid Sister? 38
Confronted by My Perfect Self 39
From a Large Green Plant 40
In Response to Your Complaint 41
To Windsor Apartments Senior
Citizen Housing 42
To a Lucky Horse 43
O David 44

PART 2 .... **47**
  Patience to Fortitude 49
  I Wish They All Could Be
  New York City Girls 50
  Thank You, Cleopatra, for Kass 51
  Hail Holy Bird 52
  Annunciation 53
  To You Black Boy From Me
  White Boy 54
  To My Baby 55
  Review of Hamlet as a Baseball
  Umpire Trainee 56
  Trespassers 57
  Dear July 4 John 58
  To the Army 59
  Welcome, American Confederacy 60
  What Are You 61
  Give Me Your Tired, Your Poor 62
  Letter to the Editor 63
  Yet One More Love Story 64
  It's Your Fault I Had to Buy Windex
  Book Club 65 66
  In Which Smokey the Bear Writes
  a Fan Letter to Winnie the Pooh 67
  To a Beautiful Woman Pooping 68
  So, You Think You're Special? 69

Asshole Rainbow 70
Warning Label 71
To an 18 Year Old Girl 72
My Sex Fantasy for Four 73
Bug 74
To a Snail by My Garden Window 75
A Woman Needs a Man Like a Fish
Needs a Bicycle 76
What Are We Men Good For? 77
To a Saint 78
What House-Cleaning People Talk
About in the Car on Their Way
to the Next House 79
For All the Real Women, To I-95 80
On the Phone with a Bureaucrat 81
If It's an It, You Know What You
Can Do With It 82
To a Piece of Meat 83
Señora Mia 84
Your Old Hands in Mine 85
O My Darling Breezy Point 86
Angie Can't You Just, Stop It!
Please? 87
Peach for My Sister 88
And All That Jazz 89
To the Reader 90

Biographical Note.................... 91

AUTHOR'S PRERAMBLE

to an Epistolary Pretense

I Want My Teddy Bear

It had clear plastic eyes with black pupils. Slowly one eye fell off, and a hole developed in the fur. Same thing happened to the rest of my family. Toys all gone. Neighborhood still there but no neighbors. The only home I can go back to is a lost war, a state of mind. So the only way I can show you my teddy bear is to talk about it.

Which is not to say this is all about me: most of the "I's" here enclosed are not myself, but personas. Here is more fiction than not, often disguised as autobiography. Nevertheless I'm getting old, and even though aging is the slowest form of embarrassment, I must risk here the personal for the sake of the universal. I hate long good-byes, but they do at least confetti the way for deathbed testimony. For the world, by way of its koalas, Teddy Roosevelts, and Poohs, I do now bare witness for a stuffed doll who cannot speak.

And that's why these poems have their epistolary pretense, to grant all from private lyric to cosmic mind an incarnation as witness to encounter: dialogue. Art is illusion—sue me. But you could do worse than sue me, as I'm convinced you're not going to read this stupid book. I say "stupid" not in self-deprecation, but as one might ask, who'll eat this stupid pot-roast, if no one's hungry? The pot-roast isn't stupid of course, but rather suffers the lameness of its circumstance. Yet, misplaced modifiers are keepsakes, for they are never lost on anyone.

Why I Don't Enter Contests or Apply for Grants

Confession: when writing, I have not the slightest idea what "good" is, because how should I care with no sense of who you are or what you want? Still, the sun rises, and somehow I have not quite set. Perhaps I am begging to fail, not having even attempted to please. But with no readers offering me the tyranny of their wishes, I've simply never learned the culture of your pleasure. I have even lost faith in J.D. Salinger's "fat lady," his spirit ear in "Franny and Zooey," the listening Jesus on the porch in the writer's mind's eye. I wander into her dreams of fatness and thinness no longer: I dream alone. If she and I went out on a date, all I could offer her is my same old teddy bear: it would be an awkward date, and would take patience.

Once upon a time I did enter contests and apply for grants, but only half-heartedly, so maybe I didn't give it enough of a chance. Why not? Oh, maybe personal baggage. My father was a terrific athlete; religion of his youth: healthy mind in healthy body, body the temple of the soul. He competed track and field, and successfully, accumulating a trunk of ribboned trophies. In the attic. There are poets who traffic in publication counts. It's about tally, about score. Just like my father. In the attic.

Then again, experience has yielded me other issues. One judge complained my work was too "chatty," and did not look like I had bothered to re-write anything. Well, let me offer some literary criticism of his rejection slip. For one thing, why is chatty bad? I have spent years training myself to be chatty on command: it can be a valuable rhetorical instrument. And why is it anyone else's business what re-writing I've done? Who is this boss I'm supposed to look busy for? I do beat out Frankenstein on hiding my monster's sutures: to my credit a critic can't see them. Another rejecter complained my work was "too loud," that poetry should be "quiet." That's like telling John Philip Souza, "Hey John, you're sharp, but you really need to lose those horns and take on violas." Congratulations, Mr. Critic, on personally preferring chamber music over marching band, but—relevance? I can't get it out of my head that the worst gang violence takes place in the poorest neighborhoods. Poetry critics all too often are either poets themselves who want you to fail unless they can ride your success, or who magically wish for you to write their own perfect poems for them.

I have a fine friend, a most excellent writer, who has won grants with good solid work. But he'd wisely held back his best—it would've been too good for them, and he'd have lost out. If I don't lack his conviction, I do lack his range; and so, while I wish more power to him, I cannot so posture myself selectively for what grants people call an emerging young artist, even in my old age.

How I Wrote and What I Wrote For

Many years ago in the *Saturday Review*, poetry editor John Ciardi wrote a column describing how he selected the poems to be published. He made a pile of the timely submissions, and began reading them, except he'd read only the first line of each. If the line didn't work for him, the poem was rejected, if it worked, it went on the reconsider pile. Thence he ploughed on through that reconsider pile, next line by next, and thence one next pile to the next, till all that remained were the elect for the upcoming issue. Is this any way to run an art form? Well, I'll grant it's limited, and in the history of literature would leave much good stuff on the editing room floor. Yet, it's efficient to the local purpose. Sometimes you have to act locally and let the globally take care of itself.

Fact: more poems get written than there'll ever be readers for. Even so for these at hand. For each included, two were written. For each written, two equally good ideas had waited in the wings, one necessarily in vain. Monty Python said it best in their ironic "Every Sperm is Sacred" song, in their movie "The Meaning of Life." In life on Earth, it is not possible for every sperm, or egg, to be sacred: the math simply won't sustain it. Most children must die. Check out Darwin. Most loaves cast upon waters never catch the eye of Pharaoh's daughter. It's the lucky Moses who lives to part anything.

Thus, for this present, I've taken on John Ciardi as my local hero. I have tried to select for lines that are crisp, and immediately available. I have striven not to be deep. "Deep" is a euphemism for "buried," and burial is for the dead. If my work dies young, let the grave be fast and shallow, because the weight of the body will not depend on archeological horizons of clay. I am not literary, not a writer so much as a sculptor who happens to dab and carve in words instead of clay. I hate the scholastic concept of "levels." You could say I'm motivated on a deeper level, but please don't.

Pardon My French

In 5th grade they teach never start sentences with "and" or "but," and always include a verb. (And never split an infinitive, till the OED recently trashed that.) Well, I break all the rules I learned in 5th grade with—no, not wild, but controlled—abandon. That's because I graduated (cum sorta) from 5th grade, and now know how. And this will be to my point: I believe in rules, and that every grade schooler should learn them.

Why is authoritarianism ever popular in the human race? Because freedom is a burden needing management. Everyone wants to be free, but no one wants loss of control, as that's scary and dangerous. Like holding your liquor. Like love is not just to have but to hold. (Okay I'm pushing?) But there are two kinds of rules: those you obey, and those you live by. Traffic lights. Stop at red, go at green. This kind you obey. Don't think, just obey. Stay alive. But how about staying up past your bedtime, or not keeping the Sabbath, or starting a sentence with "Because?" Such rules are not finally for obeying, but for compass: they tell where you are. Make you a map. Go anywhere you want, just have a map whose fat short outlined arrow reads: you are here. Old saying: rules are made to be broken. I say we live not by bread alone but by its breaking.

I write in free verse, as most of my generation. See how free we are from regular meter and rhyme? But: an irony. Regular meter and rhyme is actually easier than free verse, as the rules limit you to more manageable choices, organizing for you. In free verse, your freedom forces more decisions on you. So it's not from laziness I write free verse, rather a bowing before the demands of the modern cultural ear (Oh, demands at last from a kind stranger, take my arm!), whose taste for the stuff seems momentarily dedicated. Purists will claim the world is going to hell, but I don't think we eggs can choose our hand-basket. All I know is English is bad French on top of bad German. And French is bad Latin and some bad Greek. And German, Latin and Greek are all bad Indo-European. And now here I am, breaking the rules of American English, which is bad British. I'm bad.

Truth, Justice, and My Way

Always tell the truth. (Except when monsters corner you, then lie.) Artists can learn this lesson from their dogs and cats. Tell your truth, and you are more than nothing; lie, and you are less. Only if you don't exist may you be simply nothing. Dogs and cats can't lie: they therefore are always by nature more than nothing, prospering in the given of their being. To be a true artist, be a dog or a cat.

People love half-truths, the convenient halves. Like: men and women are unfaithful. True? Sure. But, they are both faithful also. So goes political propaganda.

Truth is popular, but only the fun and handy half. The problem with truth is the whole truth, wholeness threatening to be a house of cards divided against itself. If what I attempt in these pages offends a reader, I am sorry, for I am truly not hostile; yet I am not sorry enough to abandon and forsake a truth's wholeness.

I am a child of the '60's and '70's, the sexual revolution, advent of the Pill's invention and consequent rediscovery of the clitoris. Columbus, you blew your chance at greatness on pillaging. Gold? Better to let the selfishness of earth plough itself forth into the generosity of flowers. Granted I'm a hold-out romantic flower child, but I have never given in to the sentimentality of Valentine's Day cards: I don't talk dirty. Real feelings are strong, wild, complex, confusing, scary. Sentimentalize them and they get modest, simple, predictable, gift-wrapped, safe. I sincerely believe this is why so many people talk dirty: they're playing the safe sentimentality card. But while my generation largely sinks inexorably, as most, into becoming its parents, its burning wisdoms suffering toward ashes, I am blessed with the curse of having no home to return to. I remain young at heart if only because I have no old age to hide in.

You're a poet? Yes. And your university position? Then, when my answer is none, the blimp covering the sports event crashes. Oh, so you're not really a league player, says the face, deflating. Long ago, when I was lucky enough to score poems with the *New Yorker*, the question came up, where did I go to school? School of what?—I thought. Lark Ellen, West Covina, CA?, PS 98, Queens, NY?, Hard Knox, Milky Way? There's an academia problem here. I must say that in my personal experience with poetry editor Howard Moss, at the *New Yorker*, that I was well treated. I enjoyed their high standards, and remain grateful for that. But for poets in general it's an ecological niche deal. Deer run wild in the woods and fields, but dairy cows need to yield milk to humans, or go extinct.

For poets, in my time and place, there is no marketplace, unless you're lucky in your political moment wave. Like being black, female, poor or gay. Coming of age in the '60's and '70's as a white hetero man from the suburbs with no musical gift, I was dead. Except for the Vietnam War. Draft age. Bingo, except alas I was too late a bloomer to either be or milk that cow. I could have been a spoilsport and envy those in dictatorships, where you might die to let a pin drop, instead of living a death out here in democracy where no one hears a bomb drop. But no, I just wandered off and decided poetry is really just about communications, more like being in advertising than school. In that case, what object to satisfy? If not a tradition, or even a market? How about an ear? Not that of the "fat lady," but a real one out there? What is the shape of a listener's ear? How goes the landscape of a Georgia O'keefe painting: bone and flower? What may my poet serve: carrion or nectar?

I look at two kinds of successful artist: those who think more like everybody else than anybody else, like Bob Dylan, and those who are really nuts but get historically lucky, like Walt Whitman. By the way, I like both those guys. So why am I a worldly failure, instead of a Bob Dylan or Walt Whitman? Maybe I just don't think straight. Unlike Dylan, I don't think more like others than most others, and unlike Whitman, I have not been faithful to one crazy bride, but rather played a blurry field. Question: if a writer crashes on a desert island, and the coconut tree does not drop a coconut, did the writer make a sound? Or does the sea remain his only emergency flotation device?

PART 1

Ah Sunflower

You are blooming even above the tassels of my corn,
sun shining in the sun.
But you are not weary of time.
Only I am,
having lost count of my own steps.
Ah, sunflower, innocent of your own becoming,
I am your God, planter of the seed that bore you, guardian now, and
collector of your seed in its turn.
Yet
my hands of clay
humble me before you,
break my heart in weakness before your glory.
When the tears of Adam and Eve washed Eden from their eyes,
was it their God,
more than they, who walked out
into the wilderness?

Apology to Karen

Fact
is millions of women would kill to have a man who does
laundry.
The fact that I have
just hung out the laundry on the backyard line to
dry at 3 a.m. is not an act of
obsession:
I simply can't sleep. So, in desperation I've made myself useful—
a shame it takes desperation, granted
I woke you but
at least I
was quiet enough so no one called the cops.
Imagine:
"Officer, just because
I am in my nightie at 3 a.m. in my dewy backyard does not mean I am
raping and pillaging, I am armed only with clothespins,
Sir."
Karen, I'm sorry
I woke you with my wakefulness. In your anger as you kicked me
the laundry basket, you called me a crazy man.
Well, what else would you
have?
A blockhead of cement, who has no soul?
And doesn't even do
laundry?

To the Gordian Knot

What is a knot
not
but self-loving splendor?
Slithering against yourself, could you untie yourself?
Or is that just not a lover's problem?
Be
fruitful and multiply!
And indeed you are fruit that pullulates paths of self-possession.
But, in serving, fruit must soften and fall,
yield
up sweet tears to whatever
drinks love's embrace back to simplicity, as knothead Alexander,
cleaving you asunder,
plucked the heart of plunder for his
doom.
So I,
no cut above, softened and cut to the quick by time,
do ask, one knotty fruit to another,
Sweetie, will you be
mine?

To My Digestive Tract

Sometimes,
daring the stillness of whatever still moment openly lurks,
you make noises that are almost
human.
Imagine that
you are the soul of a child never born? Of a roasted chicken torn
from its tomorrow?
Voice crying in the wilderness of
everything I am?
Tell,
flesh made spirit, of the Great Beyond, proclaimed
Kingdom of Heaven
within,
and speaking in tongues of gut feeling,
are you oracle, cryptically making plain the way to disembowl
Persians? Or, have I just
missed my last
pill?
Sometimes
you sound like my cat.
Don't you dare have a hairball!

Sir Dinner

Ahem!
Stop talking back there, please. Thank you.
We are gathered for a special feast.
Our guest
of honor is our missionary.
He has worked so hard to convert us, with all heart, and some success.
Two regrets:
he will not get to share repasting with us tonight, and
alas, we are still
cannibals.
But at least we've learned to show gratitude to the Lord, for a bounty
we are about to receive.
Therefore,
Sir,
if you will be kind enough to say Grace,
before stepping into the
cauldron?

Jack as the Being Stalked

You want my cow in exchange for a handful of magic beans?
Okay.
(Yes, I'm stupid.)
So I planted them, and next morning
a deep canyon appeared next to our cottage. "Stupid kid," Mom said,
but then she always did.
Turned out the magic beans contained a soil fungus that digested the
whole planet!
Big deal, I never thought the place looked great anyway.
But Mom insisted on dinner, so
down I went
into the bottomless pit of dark life.
Down there lived a giant who said, "Take what you want, it's all
covered with greasy black stuff anyway."
So I did,
and me and Mom made a killing on heirloom furniture.
Of course drillers got the oil.
(Mom and I are stupid.)
So,
I'm here to buy our cow back.
We're offering you a mahogany desk and swivel chair, extra large.
Yeah, they've been degreased. We'll even throw in
a bonus clean
pelican.

Bob Dylan's X-Mas Album
(a review)

Dear Bob,

Thank you.
You've just made it easier to keep Christ in Christmas.
Or harder: how do you manage to keep it all hid
in plain sight?
Dear Landlord should have provided you with a working
shower to record this one in, with White Noise for backup, or back
out.
This Christmas
you have gifted me with the immaculately frightful joy
of standing motionless, jaw drooled to the floor, repeating, "I just can
not believe it's that bad, just can't grasp it's…"
It's almost enough to get me knock knock knockin' on
Heaven's door
because,
it being impossible to wreak such a deed on purpose,
either cosmic accident prevailed or
God is great.
I gotta hand it to you, as in cash, because—not wanting to be so
all alone—I once again robotically turn to go and buy your album.
Congratulations!
From one who can sell nothing,
you can sell anything.

So a Fly Lands on Your

Stove,
right on the oven-on button.
You swat the fly, killing it and turning
the oven on.
Who
could anticipate that killing a fly would have the consequence of
turning an oven on?
What? Kind of a universe is this?
Turns out
there's an element that if you get enough of it
concentrated in one place it'll—
look it up, I'm not making this up—just go and blow itself and every
thing up!
Out of all proportion to anything credible and all on its own
for no damn good reason.
Maybe this is true too for concentrated people?
Fire is good for cooking supper but
maybe
you and I should
avoid armed concentration.
We wouldn't want to butt each other's buttons by sorry and blow
up.

To the Fly I Just Killed

You died so well.
And, I think, of course, flies are good at dying—experienced
expert droppers, leading the
Way.
But then,
I reconsider: you are descended from a line of
life continuous unbroken for four billion years. Like me, last time
you did not exist as life, God's face
had not yet shone upon
waters.
So, after all this time, I bet you were
really out of practice, after
all.
Well, nothing like getting whipped back into shape! Maybe
you'll return as a guru on a mountaintop and
teach me the
Way.

Take Me Out at the Ball Game

What?
do you mean
you don't feel like crossing Home Plate?
Look, you
hit the ball over the fence, you're the winning run: come home!
Then, if it sweetens the heart of your
cute bottom, go
home.
How can you just not happen to feel like it?
You owe it to your team, your employers, your fans.
All you can do is shrug at me?
Don't you
have any integrity or pride? Oh, just not right now.
So, you're gonna just pitch a tent here at 3rd base? That's not my kind
of pitching—I call that too underhanded even for
hardball.
A new contract offer
won't swing it? So you won't play ball for the money thing, then.
I can't believe it's just a mood issue.
Oh really, so it's you need to belong to yourself first, aha!
You're not gonna let this
world walk all over you and tell you
what to be?
Well, dammit, you're sure
walking all over
me!

Never Let

Never
let anyone else tell you who you are.
Let others teach you, reach your mind and heart, but never
let anyone else tell you who you are.

Always know
there is no one you can't learn from, for the day you decide
       another is just ignorant, that day your soul will invite its own
       ignorance in, and begin to die.

Only never let anyone else tell you who you are.
Not man or woman,
not white or black, nor any nation or creed, nor the powerful or weak,
       nor age, nor the dead speaking out of history.
Save this last job for yourself:
tell yourself who you are.

Let not even love compromise you past halfway (we need love
or we can't win) as even true lovers suffer the sincerity of whoever
they can only but be. But
never
let anyone else tell you who you are.
Tell yourself who you are,
or burn in the hearth of another's convenience.

Dear Clement C. Moore

I am just a wee bit
pissed off
at your Christmas poem about my visiting your house
that night a few years back.
Centuries I've striven to keep my service at a low key. And now your
"Visit
from Saint Nicolas"
anchor around my neck has burdened me into stardom.
"Not a creature was stirring, not even a mouse?"
I wish
only that it could have been a mouse instead of you!
And after that movie, "Miracle on 34th Street,"
I can't go anywhere.
And now with global warming I can't even stay home.
Between you
and those Coca-Cola ads, working me up big and red, the gropies think
my pants are filled with toys.
Ach!
The brandy, please.
May your mice claim your cookies.

To Poe or Not to Poe

That
is my question.
Do I even want to talk to you? After all your horrible talk
against ravens?
In a previous life I was that raven.
So?
How could I know what I was saying?
Lenore this or Lenore that? I've never even known a Lenore.
Like, I'm a human now, this time around, and I work in a laundry.
I have enough problems;
leaky machines,
I'm divorced and my grown son won't speak to me,
and the dryer noise drives me nuts, and I'm supposed to care about a
creepy old guy whose wife died? God
rest her
soul, of course, I feel your loss, but now do I also need
your blame for tapping and rapping on windows just because once,
upon being a raven, I incidentally landed on this
crybaby's
stupid and pathetically sacred so-called plutonian shore?
So it was a dark and stormy night.
So?
I swear I'd never've done it if I could've helped it. Now,
thanks to you, I can but dream of
Nevermore.

Mom

Mom.
I need to love you.
Fortunately I can, but why?
You had me on purpose, against all medical advice.
Yet, I was an accident
because I should not have been.
Because of your tuberculosis, having me angered your infectiveness
back to life, killing my sister and you.
Your heart was in the right place, but your choice wasn't.
I alone
have lived to tell the tale:
My children walk the earth and not my sister's.
I don't feel guilty.
I feel broken hearted.
Whenever I look at a butterfly, or an oak tree, I think
how magnificent, in every way beautiful… but also how lonely and
lost in the vast ashes
of the stars.
Mother who gave me life, thinking of you,
so I think.
But I cannot thank you for life—
only for loving me.
Sorry.

Dad

How come
You turned out to be such an asshole?
And I such a weakling?
You
such a hero, athletic tough hearted worker.
I
such a lovely child.
Yet, after the way of mom and sister, I abandoned you
when all you had to have done was let go, and you'd have had me for
keeps.
And all I had to do was grow
around you: entirely surrounded by son, you'd have happily aged into
tameness, on your
pedestal. But
no,
you were not man enough to let me become a man.
And I was not man enough to stop being a boy regardless.
Was asshole and weakling
the best we could
be?
We should have been worth each other's love.
Or loved despite unworthiness.

To Chicken Dinner

In the Beginning God lived in the World,
rose up
from rocks, roots of trees, flowered and fruited into
Us.
All of us. But now
God has His address in Heaven,
works out of an air conditioned high-rise, makes business trips
down here only if it's really important corporately.
(Some say he sends his Son the Doctor down on
house calls.)
Today
when we seat ourselves to eat you,
we thank the Lord above, our Father in Heaven,
even though you're the one
doing all the
dying.
Chicken, whom we are about to receive,
ten thousand years ago
we thanked
you.

Doomsday, What's Your Angle?

How can we prepare?
Bible says mostly we'll be caught off guard, meaning
biblical warnings must
fail
in order that they be fulfilled.
Meaning Hell and Heaven are in bed together, and you, Doomsday,
are the bed.
Admit it does come off whiffing a bit of class warfare—
supporting cast of expendable thousands, eh?
What's your next gig, Horseman
of the Apocalypse,
stud farm duty? Ah, all those bomb-shell eternal night
mares to service… but, Mr. Dreamboat,
back down
here you're just a one trick pony
one time event we can't learn from, a cosmic high to get high for. Like
smoking dope to watch a total eclipse.
Hey save it for when there's
not one.
Love
is exactly the wrong moment for special effects.
Do you love me, O Doomsday?
In my life I have been the least effective evil person I've ever known.
So, in advance, I offer you my contrition and tears:
Judgment
will likely catch me eating a muffin and
sipping herbal tea.

Dear Birth

Ew!
Keep your paws off me.
I just can't
stand bright lights and icky sticky and all
sudden hot and cold and
Eyes! World used to be looking everywhere and now it's all on
Me.
You're making me want
to be beautiful and delicious.
Stop it stop it if I'm beautiful and delicious eyes will
eat me.
Must you tease me with a silver lining on sorrow?
You are beating me up by making me have
what I must lose.
Why?

Dear Death

Kill me already.
Oh, I keep forgetting: you don't take
orders.
I keep hoping you're a waitress, "I think I'll have a Quick Oh!
-blivion, well done, and maybe a moment of
ecstatic near
You.
Thank you. No, that will be all."
Instead, it's one
piece at a time: teeth, eyes, hair, muscles, stomach, joints, mind, sex—
what am I, a 7 cities of Troy reunion party?
Are you making fun of me? I play Daffy Duck to your
Bugs Bunny.
Why?
Oh, I keep forgetting, since you are Nature, there is no why. So I'm
guessing you're the reason most would rather trust in a
loving God who
kills.
Alas, unlike Easter
eggs, the parts you hide won't be found
uncracked behind curtains.
My Easter's over.
Is the shape of my pain your only available face? If only you were
despicable.
But you haven't even mind enough for cruelty.
I hate you, for you do what you do not even by reason of
insanity.

Hey Canada Geese, How Come Your Babies Almost Never Get Run Over Anymore?

Every Spring there you are, your fuzzy buff goslings in obedient tow,
feeding in the grassy drainage ditch by my roadside.
Year after year.
And years ago,
when you were new parents, there'd be sad fuzzy buff bumpies
on my road; but hardly ever any more.
You learned to be good parents,
teach your children what
you know.
Except, we humans can't.
While most of you arise by wise adults, seasoned on many seasons,
we get raised by raw near-children.
Humans mostly have but one shot parenting, then
we're shot.
Like you, we learn to keep them off the road, but often
not in time. Like yours, our wisdom grows, but ours grows only old,
and with us dies.
Why did the human cross the road,
only to become a sad fuzzy bumpy, for nothing
on the other side?

Advice to Parents

Shut up.
You talk too much.
You just keep repeating your speeches over and over.
What, are you trying to be immortal or something?
But wait.
You should speech.
We kids are thus rightly being programmed for when we have kids.
Thank you for obnoxious utility.
But—
and it's a big fat butt
in your face where it belongs, hope you can back your
kiss off enough to
smile?—
smile you must, at the camera of immortality. Ha!
Gotcha.
We'll crop the image later.
Childhood is Hell.
We grow up as an act of self defense.
And we'll grow up overweight on top of you if you don't watch out!
Yet, I'm so so sorry.
I know you hurt.
And you tried.
And you're only what you are.
Just know that we remember, and that we surely will slap
immortality in your
face
after you die.

Hey Fat Old Man

Nobody
wants to see you,
so you need to get real and go for that invisibility look:
appropriate is the new fashionable.
Remember
how women pretended not to notice you,
dimming their lights to keep it cool? Really made you feel
like Somebody,
huh?
Forget about it!
You're ugly now—so ugly's your game in town.
I'd do rumpled mismatched clothing, not so clean, and don't shave.
(But no beard,
or you might, horrors, pass for counter-culture dignified.)
If you have a wife
(God
has blessed you.) then wear her hand-me-downs.
Shoot for that haute couture it's-all-over glow, with highlights of
canny je n'existe
pas.
Heads in droves will not turn,
eye contact will be with whoever is standing behind you.
Rob a bank:
witnesses will say, "Yes, officer, he… well, let me think… he
had on a… um, gee…" And you're
scott free!
So be like me, because freedom is wherever it slams you,
because it just happens that the fat old
nobody is the new
Somebody.

To an Artist as a Young Not Somebody Yet

Hey
you suck
up to cheese
fizz aerosol milky cosmic way nozzle and root
root root for the cash flow
nipple right now kid
or else
you are refusing to be the mammal you are, and that's an order
to maintain the integrity of your survival, by sucking
while you're still a baby which you are.
Yes,
know your purposes and your methods for their giftly demands
but
distinguish between integrity and purity.
Know nobody will ever love you for your purity, for heaven's sake,
much less pay you for it, because the fizz aerosol milky
cosmic way nozzle and root world offers
only love and money
in exchange for the same coin so
sell out!
You think you're above the working class?
Integrity—look it up—means staying in one piece.
Sex workers go out and sell nothing of themselves but service,
and come back home weighing
the same.
Love waits in the wings you fly on.
So how about not too heavy but just weigh in, and that's an order
of magnitude brighter
for a
Star.

O Cat

Thou
of the most
magnificent accident of history, and fountainhead of your absolute
identity—Oh! That you should be mine and
own me.
You
sleep in my presence
with such sprawling and languid trust I could easily kill you
and yet I don't
even annoy you if I can help it. Instead I
serve you. Are you
smart?
Or just stupid and lucky?
You are tucked into a magic nook in the human race,
which includes the back-yard and the front-yard and, unfortunately
driveways.
You are spayed and doomed.
Welcome, O cat, and
prosper.

Welcome, Plants and Animals That I Eat

Pardon me for interrupting
your whatever
but I feel the need of telling you where you live:
me.
I
am your ecological niche.
My hungry mouth is your
forests, your grasslands, your tundra, your wetlands, your mountains,
oceans, lakes, rivers, wilderness and garden.
If I die, you go extinct.
Sorry.
(Okay not overly sorry—my heart that does go out to you is
not a Saint's.)
But even if our Planet had all the wild places it once did,
you couldn't make it there, not anymore.
Ain't evolution a bitch. (Hey,
I'm forced to know we all die, and you're not. So
that joke's on me.)
Deal:
you give me
your tired, poor huddled masses yearning to breathe free, and
I give you a safe place to
lay your eggs.

To Fear

I have nothing
to fear
but you? Little old you. Merest wisp of
everything real.
It's not that I haven't tried in my life
to do well despite whatever.
Hope.
Valor.
Fist in the sky, yeah: sic 'em with Whatever Power!
I've always done my best but you've
taught me better, story of my life the story of bad dreams
coming true.
Santa
Claus from Hell,
pulled by reindeer skeletons,
sack full of anti-toys, dark blotches that suck up
and away toys I once had.
Bullies
in the schoolyard, death in the family, loss of lots of
teeth! As in I really brushed and yet
virtue did not
help.
Nightmare bullies and deaths and lost teeth all replaced
by the real thing.
Hey I'm not complaining to the world's
Whatever-and-Virtue Council about my pain: I can
see
the magnitude beyond myself.
I just want to bear witness to the price of bearing
witness—Fear, have I created you or
you me?

To a Corpse with the Hiccups

Try
shutting up?
I'd tell you to drink a glass of water and hold your breath but
well, look at you.
I bet cremation would've shut you up.
At least you're not farting.
Incurable,
that's what you always were,
carrying humanity to a fault, like a foundling
to a doorstep with a
padlocked door.
So now you've given up the ghost, but not the hiccups.
It's embarrassing
in such a quiet room—you're jolting the flowers, and the children
are giggling through their fascinated dread.
Adults
keep checking their watches; better you'd
swallowed a ticking clock.
Or bomb.
A bomb would be just like you.

And So, Fidel

Castro!
Yeah you, of Cuba fame.
The Great Aging One, you're not dead yet?
You know, for a smart guy you still don't seem to have figured out
that the final greatest act of a revolutionary
is to die.
So you owe us: you've been holding out on us.
No hostility intended.
Not personal.
Look, you did a great thing.
(Cuban missile crisis? Oh dear, bad boy moment! Yet we
all got away with it, so cool.) But
getting back to death: Die.
Let go.
A revolution that can't survive its creator is a failure.
Look at Jesus, for Christ's sake.
Poor bastard
(and he was one: God and Mary weren't married) probably didn't
even believe in God, and yet, see?
Come on, Fidel.
If it can't stop being about you, it can't start
being about the rest of us.

O My Sweet-Heart Statue of Liberty

I was once inside your head.
Long ago.
And literally too, as a tourist.
A young man then, I was full of promise but, you know how
promises can break when they
fall on hard
times.
Still, I really have tried to stay faithful to you, even though
I find myself now in later life
tired and poor,
my wretched mass often huddling. Okay so I don't
teem on a shore—must I be
perfect?
Will you keep the love-light burning, and let me call you sweet-heart?
I am in love with you, even though it scares me
how hollow you can be.
But,
then, it is my task to hoist the old heavy vow
to help make you full.

Back

Dad?
Yeah?
Why do I have a back?
Go to sleep.
No, really, why is it back there?
Where else would it be? And something's gotta be back there.
Why?
Because you've got a front, a chest, and so forth.
Well, then, why do I have a front?
Because fronts are good, I guess.
What are fronts good for?
They defend and move everything else forward.
Including the back?
Yeah.
So the front is for the back.
Yeah, I guess.
So what's the back for?
Go to sleep, son.
I'm not tired.
I am.

Dad?

Yes son?
I just got the sudden feeling someone's listening in on us.
We're alone, son, go to sleep.
Who could it be?
God.
Somebody besides God.
Maybe they're God but don't know it?
Hmm…
Besides, how could you feel someone was listening
before we even started talking?
Maybe they could sense we were about to.
But we wouldn't have been about to without your sudden feeling.
So, does that mean I'm to blame?
Son?
Yes dad?
Let's go to sleep. Then they'll get bored and go away.
If they're ghosts, would it help
to hide under the sheet?
Yes.

Dear Robert B.

Okay.
It's come down to it after all these years.
I should have apologized to you.
Right off.
Basic.
Oh sure it pissed me off in the 8th grade that you'd lost—lost?—your
virginity
while I had to wait years,
and far too many before I got to split
and cast off the tight old spent skin of my own
failure to
grow.
I should
have had the social skill to simply say sorry for an incidental affront.
And you should
have had the social skill to do other than wrestle me down
after school on somebody's lawn, extracting
contrition,
patent insincerity trophy.
We were two bright school-mates
who flunked that
course.

Patti Dear?

What
was that
in all so-called creation all about?
After long pleasant casual acquaintanceship in the work-place,
"Good! Good! Good!" you
shouted,
pumping your arms in triumph in the hall, when I dropped
an armload of books on the stairwell.
Days it took
my bewilderment to fade, before inrushing hurt and anger.
What
was it that caused you to
hate me so much
that at our every crossing I got seething holy hatred in your eyes?
I dared not touch you even with civility of speech.
My shrink said I must've done something.
Something.
Was it the time I scratched an itch
in my ear?
You could have said something I could hear.
I never even remotely came on to you, not even politely.
Was that it? I snubbed you with respect?
I grasp at hollow straws
you leave me.

Oh! Liana

I have not thought of you in decades.
Even back in youth I never felt much in the way of physical
desire for you.
We never dated, never
went out,
were just incidental friends who shared a job situation.
Closest we got was dinner at your place, and a letter I mailed you—
unanswered—after I got married to somebody very
else.
Yet
this morning I awoke (I
sure did—haven't slept since) with you
you, vividly, I mean like totally viscerally in my
out of my
mind.
I could not stop us from being passionate hot and heavy lovers.
I could not stop smelling and tasting you to death
(mine) after 40 years of nothing.
Sorry
about the delay.
How did I not know?
How did I not know?
Oh Liana,
I should have known
I should have known to risk failing you for one moment, that I might
have done right by you in the fullness
of so much empty
time.

Liana, Again

On second thought—was there a first?
(Do thoughts snap to?)
maybe
after 40 years
we should not meet again.
Not that ever realistically we might, but posed just as a thought
experiment, like curved space: empty
yet in thrall to
gravity.
"What a relief," my imaginary you thinks.
Recently I chanced upon a woman I'd not seen in only 20 years,
(Only?
Oh good Lord! 20 years has now
Become an Only?) one who'd weighed in my imagination well, though
not in life beyond one lightest kiss—even so,
I did not know her
face.
I was crushed by her still knowing mine.
Would I know your face now, Liana? I fear how you
has sunk to just a
thought.

Why, Stupid Sister?

Caroline, you 're a bitter pill.
Why
did you not take your medicines?
Nobody there to make you?
The drawer by your bedside was filled with untaken pills when you came home to die.
Did you
hate somebody or something, or just your mindless 14 year old
self?
I, your kid brother, when 14,
was not mindless—your example had trained me
to take bitter pills.
Thank you.
The pills
thrown out that could have saved you, are likely still in a
landfill somewhere, just like
you.
Only, in your landfill Mom's on top of you.
I don't know where Dad got put.
But the momentum of you still helps make the world go round.
If
there's a Heaven, and we meet again, I will slap you upside the head
against the hard wall of you so hard it'll make
me dizzy,
for not taking your stupid
pills.
And then I'm gonna hug
and kiss you
forever.

Confronted by My Perfect Self

You're not fair.
I could've been so much more if only I hadn't been held back
by being less.
Oh your gloves fit so so fine!
But don't all gloves fit like a glove, even if they miss
fit?
Will that I am misunderstood be my only claim
to being seen?
Why do I have to have my perfection wasted on all these stupid faults?
I would be completely different except for the unfortunate
accident of being as I am.
So everything wrong with me becomes icing
on your cake!
But
you're not perfect after all: because
you need icing.

From a Large Green Plant

You started it.
Yes you did, I didn't, middle of last night.
So our playful accusations of somnolent wee hour love making
go.
Anyway one of us came on to the other under
dream nakedness cover, and next
day
you shyly confessed that in tropic dark narcofluff I'd been to you a
large green plant.
Large green plant?
Does that mean you were cheating on me? Or, am I some
how really
a
Hey! very large other
man buster, I say step aside, 'cause I am her one and only
large green plant!

In Response to Your Complaint

When I hold you in my arms
I
can't sleep.
No, this is not a rant about your snoring.
Our first night together, as we spooning agog your bed, your eye
lashes flicking on my back kept me
sentinel
till, slipping off at last, I night
mared having four hands and four feet, and startled cried out;
the extras were
yours.
Then, once, you had your period.
The sudden sticky that time was not my fault.
A towel averted a new sheet—you were embarrassed, but I was
charmed.
I
therefore don't get why you get
so pissed off when I drop off on the couch agog the TV. Don't
you understand I'm
resting?

To Windsor Apartments
Senior Citizen Housing

So
I should come on to you?
You did offer your flyer, now that I'm, ahem, senior.
You nail it: Mt. Everest's a simple teen pimple—time to burst
youth's bubbles of boundless
troubles.
Problem
is I'm already seeing somebody: my wife.
She and I share what realtors call a home and I call a house,
in the suburbs.
For now.
Sure,
your Efficiency Handicap Accessible floorplan looks neat
at 360 sq. ft., yet
while a far cry from all the sky face of my planetary dreams, higher
truth now comes down increasingly to
decreasing
space.
Ain't love a place? Ain't it swell
how old makes thinking small the new
all?

To a Lucky Horse

You lucky horse you, that I am not
king of the world,
free
to do anything at will, beyond all limit and retribution.
Oh, I'd be a good ruler, at first.
Yessir and ma'am
I'd most circumspectly cure poverty, injustice and stuff, and
heck, why not?
Why be a bad sport?
But. But, temptation. Temptation would creep in—fact is people
are not made to be moral in a vacuum.
I
would
finally yield
to one temptation after
another and you, my dear horse.
I've always wondered what'd happen if you put a horse on roller
skates—would he glide gracefully across or
flop crazy?
If I were king of the world, I'd just have to find out.
Lucky you I'm not.

O David

David
David.
Written in stone.
They say winning isn't everything.
But the ones who say that are not the ones who have lost.
You beat me fair and square,
and today half the world is named David, and the other half is named everything else but
Goliath.
Did I not also nurse at my mother's breast?
Play with my sisters and brothers?
I kept faith and served my people, just like you, and
just like you,
would have sired a joyous plunder into righteousness! But
instead,
because, because of
an instant of sheer inches one way or the other of hurled stone,
my mother cries as I lie brain-dead and bleeding
for all time, because it is written
instead of
gone.

PART 2

Patience to Fortitude

I know
Fortitude's a Virtue,
but Fiorello LaGuardia got it wrong when, Mayor of our Fair New York,
he so named us, Lions as carved, poised astride the steps
of The Library.
Meanwhile that 11 year old girl
garbled it right when she blurted in accidental wisdom
that your name's
Attitude.
Grant please there's too few passing virgins for us to roar at in New York;
consider then what our town claims to be roared at?
Attitude!
Yeah, 'cause Patience without Attitude is Submission,
and Attitude without Patience is Abandon.
How New York.
Hey, the two of us together know how
to think twice: that's a
Library.

I Wish They All Could Be New York City Girls

I
don't
repeat don't
wish they all could be California girls.
I was born and raised in New York City, where girlitude is awesome.
Thanx
I'm welcome.
Sure you got your cute C-jobs
with the way they beam they keep their boyfriends tan all night but
Oh the humanity!
as this noseless and chinless identity-free lighter than air
person, bursting into passion, sears
the New Jersey tarmac of my
kiss?
No thanx.
Hey California guys
gimme
faces like the emigrant mountains my girls hail from,
noses goats can climb.
And attitude—oh don't get me started. Okay ignore Bronx
girls don't think Queens girls even are from NYC
but who could be
more romantic than a NYC girl with wild winds blowing through her
sarcasm?
California hail! But I'm
right
because I heard myself say so.

Thank You, Cleopatra, for Kass

Out
into the livingroom from the kitchen
to me she came,
bearing incense of smoldering cotton, as on a silver platter.
"I burned your socks," she blubbered, almost
proud, almost our first
date, almost our
last?
Because my socks got wet in the snow as we'd cavorted, girding your
Needle behind the Metropolitan Museum of Art,
and later, in her oven, she did, just for me, and successfully,
get them
dry.
The tale?
Old as the hills
you, Cleopatra, drew your stone spire from,
stuck hard as the storied sword
till the right one comes, and
stone as water
flows.

Hail Holy Bird

Call me
hopelessly laughing snot out of my nose an act of
prayer?
All is possible with God.
Hey feathered Moby, passing beyond all pale, listen.
12 going on 10, what did I know but I didn't wanna be in church?
When suddenly startling, you
started
starring among the chandelier sky on high, wild free starling
bird in church!
I needed to laugh so bad I'm glad it hit my nose
and not my crotch.
Mostly I held the pee in.
Everyone,
and I guess that includes me, pretended they, I mean we, didn't see you.
We all were just marking up'n'down kneeling time
till we could get
out.
Even the priest with eyes averted not his downward gazing rhetoric.
Good for you that priests don't tote
shotguns,
as you were not a pigeon, nor of clay
but an angel!
Wascally Roadrunner secret agent angel, saying look up.
I did not drown in snot, and so alone live
To tell the tale.

Annunciation

Awake
Awake
little beast donkey and fear not, for I am God's angel.
Hear what I bray unto you.
Tomorrow
your burden will be Mary great with child, to bear down the road
to the altar of a manger.
Bear her well, for soon you too will conceive,
while never having known a male donkey, such that one day your child
will bear Mary's own,
grown to manhood and a Prince,
upon strewn lilies set on a city called Peace that never
learns any,
so that this Prince
might feed the hunger of
beasts.

To You Black Boy From Me White Boy

I don't remember if I also ever sang that eeny-meany
miney-moh that once caught you
by the toe.
You
dangled there, in my mind, against blank twilight, so lonely looking
I felt sad, swirling
softly as a Calder mobile, or chandelier
lilting with a twitch when the rocks of the world tremble,
naked
as the day we were born.
Ah so skinny! —as you flailed your arms and one leg free,
gazing about with craned neck, and so
bewildered
you could not yet holler to be
let go.

To My Baby

You
are my own
flesh, yet I can't reach
your beauty as you sleep there, breathing softly as if the lift and sag
of your belly were a haze of horizons a
touched world could not
grasp.
Stinky waft of milk and honey
love does first and finally frustrate by being but a start.
You
are so self-huggingly delicious, how can you stand yourself?
What suns moons and stars peer over the edge of you,
wondering, "Is it safe
to rise?"

Review of Hamlet as a Baseball Umpire Trainee

Hey kid you're strong
in areas we want.
Eyes that catch each catch and throw, honest long as proverb day.
When you face-off cuss you do have that trippingly
on the tongue thing
down
but
stand up for yourself—
stuff this alas poor runner shit and for crying out loud shout yerr
out!
You care too fair about the feelings of others, feelings are
not the point. Mirror gotta say you're fairest of all
to belong to the ages
in baseball fairy-hail.
Kid, you run
from being maybe wrong, and that's
gonna kill ya.

Trespassers

Boy and girl
big enough for highschool backpacks but
I gotcha
this time by locking my gate
so you couldn't get through to the street from the woods behind my
property!
You had to turn around and bother
to violate someone
else.
I understand.
I understand how precious
it is for a child to run free through the neighborhood.
I do I do swear I've been
there.
You don't get old except by having been young.
But you guys are too old now—time is knocking on your door
to knock on mine, ask please
open.

Dear July 4 John

Tough
love? Or just
Lady Liberty faking the world's oldest
Vigil at my supermarket door, sticking out like a sore
head
in fatigued camouflage, yanking at my conscience teat for swig of
I owe another dollar to
you?
I don't like talking dirty
but if not truth to power then at least to dirty
who asked you
even for the time of day much less
clouds of you sacrificed at the shrine of national political poo?
I didn't ask you.
I got no freedom out of you.
You freely sign up, I pay.
You serve, I pay.
You ass
blow away hero vet hospital, I pay.
Now government screw what ass you got left, again I should pay?
Wind up living in cardboard too?
How about I come here with a great big clock,
you
feed my cup for what
time left
I got.

To the Army

Damn
Damn
Damn every single one of your
biblical tours of Hell's Hovel Hotel on Eden's
main drag through history
duty.
Because I'm told, and do believe, every single day, I need you, and not
dare
leave home without you or
be dead meat on the cutting edge
floor
of history's bloody movie.
We've all seen your movie, the footage of hard boots, what's
left of us if our crisp cadets, marching, sexy fragrant clean Angels of
Death that won't wash don't
win?
Damn
Damn
Damn you've got me
by the balls, and your glory, in my seed thereof, when I'm gone,
will bloom.

Welcome, American Confederacy

1865
you guys hurt for real.
Sorry about that.
Not the North's fun on the taffy-pull either.
Now?
You've turned
your pain into your candy, and granted, after first time around, baby!
ain't no takin' none away from a big
baby.
Hey sweetie, cantcha stop being such a co-dependent
addict?
Foaming at the South over wounds tasting too good to let heal?
Licking keeps you licked.
You're looking for love in all the wrong ages.
Have I ever told you I've always had a crush on Robert E. Lee?
I see him
bronze towering
cubits tall, flag-free but baring sword almighty in Washington, D.C.,
so worlds will come and grasp how we
take our own
home.
We must be strong.
No kisses please, but war is over
if you want it
sweeter.

What Are You

Doing
in my bed?
I just got up to pee and now when I come
back I find
you.
Wake up bastard! Get out of my life Oh shit you're
dead
in my bed and you're me.
Which means
I died?
Poor bastard, didn't even get to get out your
last biological
pee.

Give Me Your Tired, Your Poor

Hot babes
working out at the Y for
lacrosse, baby!
They say you guys eat your dead.
All who slave for vigor and beauty, themselves their own master,
have honor, and shine
free.
Let us raise a toast, drink to freedom.
Hydration is grapes to the wine of sweat.
Ah work-out women, slake me in the carnal knowledge of your
torch!
I crave the torrid trickle in your cleavage,
pray for breasts no larger than
God wants.
But what's free speech craving in that big block letter
PINK
across your ass?

Letter to the Editor

Outrage!
Superbowl's good clean American ritual combat
ruined by bare-breast menace.
Oh sure, football and T.V. brass apologize, but will anything be done?
We need a Warring Commission:
Conspiracy?
Or act of crazed lone breast
slinger?
Meanwhile the Liberal Establishment is in denial of the threat
that that Jackson woman shamelessly poses
for Society,
refusing to see the naked body as violent crime.
I may be a voice crying in wilderness, but dire consequences come—
roving gangs of breasts will smash glass and kick
innocent little old ladies
down,
char deeper virile men cursed with hearts already blackened.
It's time
to take American breasts back into custody, and lay them
to rest, treasured heirlooms in their Cups
of the Covenant
for their own ethic cleansing good, and spare
gawking children eternal nerve
damage.
Sincerely,
A Concerned Citizen

Yet One More Love Story

Oh, so that's your favorite love story?
Mine is
there's these 2 water molecules, see? And they're frozen face to face
inside an ice-cube.
Ugh, dread the hostility and frustration
in such a forced liaison!
But
the 2 molecules fall in love, like yay!
Joy to the world except alas the ice cube melts, and the lovers
wash away, never to
I can't say it.
The sad-ending movie works in France but not in the United States.
Hey, how about they meet again in a snowflake
on a child's
tongue?
On Christmas Day!
They remain entwined joyfully in the child's pancreas
for life.
Wanna spend the night with me at my place?
Or am I boring you.

It's Your Fault I Had to Buy Windex

For my car, Karen,
after our date.
Not
like I was paying attention to the physics at the time that we were fool
ing around in the front seat negotiating not sexual
politics but rather gear
sticks.
Bucket seats are the new bitch.
We weren't kids, but older guys, around the block,
yet I never knew till that night that steamy sex really does steam up
car windows.
Damn!
I mean sticky: Windex?
Permission is
the hardest value to achieve in one's personal life after one has learned
not to break glass.
Sex
is the world's best nonsense.
To stupid is a verb.
I still can't believe how stupid one has to be to do
the right
thing.

Book Club

You want me to join your what?
Already did that book
in college,
before decades got invented, before I started being all
I'll never again
be.
And if it meant what it meant the first time, why mean anything
else now? Why fix what works or
won't?
Well okay, times change,
and you're saying change doesn't have to be about broken?
And telling doesn't make time
a clock?
I get it, so I'll get it, 'cause
if I wanna make change, I gotta stop the buck here and
break it, hopefully thus finding
purchase in soft
cover.

In Which Smokey the Bear
Writes a Fan Letter to Winnie the Pooh

Um. Hi?
I know you're a big-ass celebrity and I'm a mere
conservation jock.
Toss, and
you win the kids, and I'm stuck punchin' forest fires.
But I just, well, I bask in your glow—hope I'm not pertrudin' inta
yer deep thoughts but I just
wondered maybe
we
uh, could like team up in your forest 'n' teach kids about fire? I mean,
you guys've done snow, flood, wind an' fog there so why
not also now
fire?
Like let's set one!
Don't get scared, not the bee tree—animal rights and all—and Kanga
would worry about Roo and bee-stings, so maybe
torch the 6 pine trees?
Rabbit and Owl would importantly manage,
besides
me an' my trusty shovel 'course'd off the blaze 'fore any real harm,
to kids a-cheerin'.
Hey, one bear to another, no pushy here:
sure we'd need Christopher Robin's approval.
Your thoughts?

To a Beautiful Woman Pooping

God you are
raising whitecaps on my hormone sea,
while your huge wagging
dog
biblically voids all
illusion, on someone's clean lawn. How can such a lovely
one as you be so full of
herself
as to stand there calmly watching her canine avatar wage evacuation?
But I guess I'm lost in Oz
where beautiful witches do poop-scoop.
I more than almost
see
your personals ad now:
HOT WOMAN CRAVES EXTRA ASSHOLE
BIG DOGS ONLY NEED APPLY.
I guess with what little you eat on your sexy figure diet
you can't make enough of
your own.

So, You Think You're Special?

You
more hurt than thou
like to think Oppressor's whip scores you
cut above on high?
Special?
Underprivileged
means only that you're not as more special than others as you think
you ought to be.
Jews,
Chosen People, special.
Till the Romans got more special.
Till the Jews got even by getting even more special by inventing
Christians.
Till Martin Luther got specialler than Catholic Rome.
Special.
On and on, all the special
empires, races, creeds, genders of special marching on.
And always the rich, of any empire, race, creed or gender
creaming all other
specials.
Now you
think you're special. I don't think you're special at all.
Want to stand out of the crowd?
Try equal.

Asshole Rainbow

Coward!
Thunderstorm that you are!
Running east away from setting sun shining thus up your dark butt,
illumining to glory your coat of many
colors
existing nowhere but within the onlooker's eye. Can't you
dare to be responsible for your
own existence,
asshole?
Can you not essay the self-respect claimed by a rock?
Ah no, you have to be like
Adam Eve Santa plus other poorly documented famed beings and
hide
your pot of gold
where any but a westward running sun won't
shine.

Warning Label

Use of this product may be harmful to your health.
Subsequent to use, future children and pets
may require in-vitro fertilization.
It is in violation of the moral code to allow underage persons
to read this label.
Store out of sight and reach of anyone who can
see or reach it.
Federal regulations provide that use of this product must comply with
federal regulations.
Federal regulations provide use of this product does not comply with
federal regulations.
Use of this product is not contrary to law, pending
conclusion of endless studies.
The manufacturer assumes no responsibility for uses inconsistent
with stipulated directions.
Directions:
Dispose of this product immediately upon purchase.
Lawful disposal procedures for this product have not been established.
Shelf-life is eternal but for best results use before doomsday.
Check our website for a description of our
other fine products.
Thank you for your patronage.

To an 18 Year Old Girl

I am an 18 year old boy.
You think I'm stupid.
I am.
Reason is because I can't get a job, and Heaven won't hire my
soul till I've
had one.
I don't get your own problem of not feeling worth something.
I walk into the room, I see you in all your glory,
and look around but don't see
me
at all.
You think I'm stupid?
I am but it's not that simple.
I am also a hall of mirrors with no face
to shine.

My Sex Fantasy for Four

Hello?
Sorry to call so late
but I was just on the line with my fantasy of you.
She
doesn't want to talk to you.
She's jealous because she thinks I mentally undress you when I'm
really mentally undressing her, who doesn't even exist and
wants me to undress her anyway.
Is your fantasy of me
bothering you
again?
I'd give him a piece of my mind except he already has one somehow.
Identity's a cup that runs over, bleeds like a
headline through pulp paper.
God, the real you is a head-case!
I like her better.
All I have to do to please her is be somebody
else.
Stop imagining him and he'll get lost.
Look, I'm sorry I can't be under 40 for you, but only under 40
for her.
I wish the four of us could be friends.

Bug

Hi.
I'm Harry.
Yeah, local guy. You're new around here, I can tell.
How come so steadfast on this wall?
You're heavy
on the vibes, I feel your magnetism but
why don't you
talk?
Can't we ignore those humans around the table below
and their stupid secret negotiations?
Can't we be friends?
Why are you so
cold?
It's almost as if you weren't
real.

To a Snail by My Garden Window

Benny Goodman
plays for me inside, where it is bright and warm,
clarinet cataract on crystal Mozart, cloyless mist,
dry air unalloyed.
Open window, my light, heat, aridity, and Benny Goodman's Mozart
gush out upon your wet cool dark, and on you,
brave snail.
You see light—the sun?
feel warmth—summer?
And that so very fine trembling—earthquake, thunder, predator?
Sadly you can't
know it's not the sun, but electric lighting, can't
know the warmth is only central heating. So how
could you ever find, in this trembling,
Benny Goodman's Mozart?
Poor humble snail,
I share your coiled shell, spiraling outward from birth, but not very far.
I too face colors I can't see,
thoughts I can't think,
tremblings I can only waywardly feel.
To be
is also to not be.

A Woman Needs a Man Like a Fish Needs a Bicycle

Sez who?
Your shirt, as you ride your bicycle past me on a romantically
sweet spring
day.
Does hostility sub for a stiffening breath of
fresh air in your inner tube
pump?
You do intimidate me: strong women
are a piece of cake;
it's the weak, fragile ones who head me for the hills.
Are you fishing for me? Or my evil twin brother, your love
to-hate dreamboat druther,
upstream
on your bike?
Alright I'll bite—you do need me
to read your
shirt.

What Are We Men Good For?

I asked my father, as a boy, does anyone like me?
Sure, he said, the neighbors do.
Why?
You do so little harm.
And so, since, I've wallowed in wistful how more loved I'd have been
if never born.
Women
are so basic, they are the Earth.
So, what is left for men but be the Sky?
Oh sure, without Sky what's Earth but a dead stone, true but
what
will the weather be?
Women are born, men must come to pass and be predicted.
Lord how we men snap to allegiant dance to whatever pretense tune
history's meat beats to forge our
cleats.
And love? Where's the all's fair?
War makes us more than we make war,
and we make peace when peace is what the weather calls
and chooses us
for.

To a Saint

Earth's
the right place for sin,
I don't know where it's likely to go better. And so,
I apologize for being such a
lousy sinner.
Sin
is like gravity, making everything, including grace, fall
into place.
Despite my being a lightweight, my idleness the devil's poor device,
what if all we sinners went on strike?
It's graveyard on your Mainstreet too when our sin mills
blow town.
Where would you saints be then?
Not
necessarily better off than the rest of us are,
even swinging on your star.
Be it ever so humble, your pedestal boasts all the comforts of home,
yet
one could do worse
than be a sinner.

What House-Cleaning People Talk About in the Car on Their Way to the Next House

Sorry but
I just never wanted to have sex with Nellie.
I'd've liked to have sex with you except you're lesbo and wouldn't
want me, me being a
guy and all
but
how was I supposed to know
you wanted to watch?
Come on, you know I'm on your side.
Did I ever tell the boss how you dropped the vacuum pipe right above
The glass heirloom and it
missed?
No.
Okay I'm lonely and you wanted to fix me up.
Thanks, and I'd'a had sex with her if I'd known it've tickled you
to watch but now Nellie's
gotten fired.
I'd have a vagina for you, Pat, if I could
but

For All the Real Women,
To I-95

Thank you.
Through the doors of your Delaware Rest Stop where I worked
they came streaming:
fat
bulbs to slim wands,
cloud-haired towers to pigtail-thatched huts of women, they came
off the highway to rest their restlessness;
pubescents to grannies,
white, black, all chocolates bronzes caramels and creams,
ample breasts, and vaster eyes to humble them.
And on, through all
forms moving.
No false
promised land of movie, mag or porn
flows with your whole real world of beautiful women.
Thank you,
I-95

On the Phone with a Bureaucrat

Yes,
I don't mind waiting.
I know you're busy, times being what they are, Post
Judgment Day, and all.
Okay.
I under—yes I stand, Statute of Limitations et cet.tra-lala, I get it,
I can't get Justice.
It's just that as the soul of a chicken people ate, I want
closure.
I demand to face my eater!
Well can't you run a search? I mean, Good God Almighty
keeps records,
no?
Okay, so it wasn't a nuclear family Sunday dinner?
Damn! Well, I couldn't have subpoenaed Norman Rockwell anyway,
but still… What? a fast four letter.. uh
food? food stain?
Chain?
Fast food chain?
Okay, good news is
Afterlife's got an auditorium that seats the ten
thousand kids who consumed me, so I can confront them.
Yes, I'm
still here. I-95 Rest Stop, was it?
Nuggets?
So it's gotta be a class-action closure because of so many chickens?
An immortal soul, and
nuggets?

If It's an It, You Know What You Can Do With It

Afraid to give away
any of
It?
Do you step on the scale before and after, see if you got
beat out of a pound by beating
It?
Don't you, you don't
get
It?
When I leave your bed I ain't got
It,
nor your silverware either. Thanks for the well spread service
dinner but I want
you
to be you because I am
me.
Are we eternally twelve years old? Tag,
somebody's
It?

To a Piece of Meat

You!
Failure!
Some gals wail
that men treat them as chunks of you.
Beautiful scrumptious you.
Yeah
Like, "I'd like to get into that piece of meat," or
Like, "Honey I'm Home,"
while often not minding to serve on that bee beasty dish.
Or being named Rose, as opposed to fair lady Cauliflower, a rose by
any other name but still a
vedge—
better than an animal? Hey meat, doncha feel justa bit
insulted?
Flesh behind broccoli on the deli line? Nannee nannee boo boo, stick
your head in headed for the
sack.
Meat on my plate, you're a failure.
You've got every virtue a lover would want
except
unlike women
you don't bite
back.

Señora Mia

Mia?
What am ay!—an ugly American?—
in free-everything buffet and bar in resort Barcelo Maya,
Yucatan peninsula, Mexico, as
you
wait on me seated
alone at my table, alone among tables set but yet untouched. Oh my
Señora, you are too
solicitous—yes, estoy bien, I really-issimo am.
Agua, por favor.
I am your only piecework al momento
in this factory, but do tengo friends and wife, just no ahora mismo here.
Somewhere,
al norte, most of us work for a living sort of like you.
Are you, or yours, alone, Señora mia?
Rain?
Dios bendiga por aviso de lluvia.
Si, una margarita doble para llevar, and thank you
for the sky.

Your Old Hands in Mine

I'd look up to you
from the valley of my five years
as you'd beat eggs with a fork in those same little glass bowls you'd set
and serve chocolate pudding in.
Mom,
how ever
did your hands—hands that lived not to know age—
whip that stiff staccato
dogs and cats possess to scratch their chins?
I've pondered this
as The Thinker, hand pedestal for chin, but omelet never came from
beating up a chin.
Now
I too beat eggs with fork in glass, as you.
Eggs break,
you died in the shadow of a young valley that I
outgrew, leaving me
hands,
now old at last, possessed of you:
mine own.

O My Darling Breezy Point

In an apartment
stuck in Bayside, excavating for a life,
lived a minor, boy of 16, and his telephone that rang.
O
teenage girl
stuck bored summer out at Breezy Point South Shore Long Island
wherever you random-dialed from for
kicks and I got kicked
into the
Hi.
And wow it we
talked I'd never talked to a girl be
leaving all awkward in silent dust we squawked and jabbered and so
innocently about every nothing I can't anymore
now.
I am wanting
just glad I didn't did I? fall in
to your calling back several times—knowing would've
drowned the hell out of my foaming
dust.
You are lost and gone for better.
Signed, No Swimmer,
Breezy Point.

Angie Can't You Just, Stop It! Please?

You giggle
after flipping out how you got raped at age 13
while boasting of your sexy legs.
You're a sweet spirit,
I can tell.
So we're sitting here contiguous cubicles phone market-survey
factory find out what folks think about the world and
you confess
with your afro-haloed tawny face whose bones
come from Ireland that you
sassed
your highschool principal into suspending you because you insisted
you're white, which you also simply are. (And
I'm thinking
bet you're glory in the sack for a white girl.)
Neighbors tossing bricks over the fence at you.
Giggle.
And you wonder why you go berzerk when you get mad, hit scream
hurl smash stuff and don't remember after?
Sweet spirit
you wanna kill kill kill you're so goddamm mad! You fuck
ing scare yourself crazy 'cause how could such a sweetie go kill?
Gotta blank out to
hide.
Please, Angie, make friends with your rage.
Please don't kill anyone innocent
like you.

Peach for My Sister

Tree
grew in waking sun
shine open back of the laundry place on the avenue
door down from funeral home
where you'd soon
lie.
Our dad
took me there
with him; while our bed sheets groaned and sighed,
he showed me God's own tree,
crescent moon leaves and hard green stones swelling toward promise
of rosy soft sweetness of my
first
first ever peach off a live tree and
while yours
was not my first funeral—grandmother's was—yours
was first to lay me down in the fruit
of a soul to keep
sleep.

And All That Jazz

Wake up jerk bird!
We all stood on deck on the prow of the New York Harbor Ferry
when all of a
you
stupid seagull, digressed.
Special jazz band music trip around happy noise
confection-glazed
Manhattan.
Satchmo all those guys aboard just loud low-ridin', and we listening
mere mortals hung on to the
railings.
We humans out front in sweet dark but sentinel
watched seagulls in front below, bobbing bath toy softly on dark wave
lets rise and scatter before us
unto slow
you
noticed us too late.
Flapping hastily you rose affront white water.
Our ship was hot on you and winning to plow you under and
then
within a foot of death
you gracefully won speed and height and
all of us humans who hate seagulls cheered go seagull! because
well, I dunno, maybe 'cause the band just gotta
play on.

To the Reader

Thank you
for reading this book.
If you're only reading this page, thanks
for that.
If you've only heard of this book, thank you for your ear's attention.
If you have no knowledge of this book but may learn someday,
thanks in advance.
If you are born and die never having heard of me,
thank you for accidentally enriching my world with your existence.
If you don't exist, never did, and never will,
thanks
for not cluttering up the place.
I'm desperate.

Biographical Note

Douglas Morea was born in 1945 in Queens, New York City, and grew up primarily there, marrying and moving to Delaware in his late 20s, where he with their mother Kass raised two daughters to successful adulthood. He remains there now with his second wife, Karen. He somehow still believes in love, and while also believing there can be too much of a good thing, he can't help but want a bit more.

www.ingramcontent.com/pod-product-compliance
Lightning Source LLC
Chambersburg PA
CBHW031257290426
44109CB00012B/618